ACKNOWLEDGMENTS

Expanding Dimensions thanks the Tarot for sharing its wisdom, for giving us guidance, and helping us grow. We would also like to thank all those who share the journey with us.

Today's Journey
TAROT

Expanding Dimensions

Illustrated by
Christopher G. Wilkey

4880 Lower Valley Road · Atglen, Pennsylvania 19310

Text by Expanding Dimensions
Illustrations by Christopher G. Wilkey

Copyright © 2011 by Expanding Dimensions
and Christopher G. Wilkey
Library of Congress Control Number: 2011928836

All rights reserved. No part of this work may be reproduced or used in any form or by any means—graphic, electronic, or mechanical, including photocopying or information storage and retrieval systems—without written permission from the publisher.

The scanning, uploading and distribution of this book or any part thereof via the Internet or via any other means without the permission of the publisher is illegal and punishable by law. Please purchase only authorized editions and do not participate in or encourage the electronic piracy of copyrighted materials.

"Schiffer," "Schiffer Publishing Ltd. & Design," and the "Design of pen and ink well" are registered trademarks of Schiffer Publishing Ltd.

Designed by RoS
ISBN: 978-0-7643-3905-9

Printed in China

Contents

Introduction
6

Keys
8 – 30

Elements
31 – 33

Fire	Water	Air	Earth
34 – 47	48 – 61	62 – 75	76 – 89

The Seven-Card Merkaba Spread
90 – 92

Conclusion
93

About Expanding Dimensions
94

About the Illustrator
95

INTRODUCTION

Artists and art lovers have known for centuries that imagery opens the mind. Pictures speak a multitude of words and also elicit emotional responses. They trigger within us a range of senses and create a union to the higher aspects of ourselves. The Tarot is based on this union, depicted in Key 6 of *Today's Journey Tarot*.

The members of Expanding Dimensions have spent years studying the Tarot. They read professionally at psychic fairs, other events, and privately for clients. Members of the group have given lectures and taught Tarot classes to others. They realized that it would be possible to incorporate the traditional structure of the classic Tarot into modern depictions that would be easily understood and yet retain the union integral to the process. With this realization, they began to create *Today's Journey Tarot*. It is easy to relate to the contemporary symbolism of this deck without struggling to understand the esoteric ideology. This leads to an illumination of the decisions needed for the future, a better perception of the present, and an understanding of the influences from the past.

If you have ever been stuck in traffic wondering if it would be better to take the next exit or stay where you are, you can read this Tarot. If you have ever known a child obsessed with video games, you can read this Tarot. If you have ever enjoyed a barbecue with friends or been worried about bills, you can read *Today's Journey Tarot*.

Every day experiences come alive with the power of archetypal imagery. The deck of seventy-eight cards includes the twenty-two Keys, traditionally depicted as the Major Arcana. The remaining fifty-six cards or Minor Arcana are divided into four suits comprised of the Elements: Fire, Water, Air, and Earth. Included within each Element is a family unit of Child, Youth, Mother, and Father. *Today's Journey Tarot* represents the true essence of the Tarot; spiritual enlightenment, transformation, and discovery as humanity expands into new dimensions.

The back design of *Today's Journey Tarot* is a merkaba, a symbolic vehicle to reach enlightenment. This symbol is repeated throughout the deck. A merkaba consists of two equally sized, interlocked tetrahedra (pyramids) with a common center, where one tetrahedron points up and the other down. "Mer" means light. "Ka" means spirit. "Ba" means body. The merkaba is a spirit body of light. It is our vehicle to expanding dimensions.

The Six of Air teaches us that today's journey is the life we lead every day. If you follow your instincts, you will always move in the right direction. Open yourself to the imagery the cards depict and trust what they convey to you. Allow this deck to be a companion on your journey.

KEYS

The Keys tell the story of the human spiritual journey. Each card from 0 through 21 is designed to portray a significant milestone on the universal quest for enlightenment, or at least to answer some of life's more fundamental questions. They incorporate archetypes that are both universally applicable, as well as unique to each individual. Archetypes are the product of the collective thoughts and beliefs of everyone who ever was or who will ever be. Archetypes are familiar signposts on our journey through the collective consciousness. Who does not cringe at the thought of the wicked stepmother or feel sorrow at the plight of the star-crossed lovers? The indigo borders of the Keys symbolize their spiritual significance.

KEY 0
BEGINNING

KEY WORDS:
JOURNEY
DISCOVERY
FAITH

The student is beginning a journey of discovery, her first deck of Tarot cards. Her expression suggests curiosity and an eagerness to learn. This is her opportunity to open herself up to a new spiritual path. The next step is her choice. She must listen to her inner voice and have faith that it will lead her in the right direction. Surrounding her are the colors that represent the four elements of nature: red, blue, yellow, and green. They suggest that she has everything she needs for her journey. She has the strength of her foundation and the potential for growth. Her cat sits confidently beside her. The cat is an animal that can see in the dark. Its presence implies that there may be more here than she is able to see.

In a reading, this card could represent a new journey, a choice, or a new beginning. It could also signify a new spiritual path or inner discovery. Faith is required to make this choice. Listen to your inner self. Seek help if necessary. Someone else may be seeing things more clearly than you.

KEY 1
MANIFESTATION

KEY WORDS:
CREATION
KNOWLEDGE
ACTION

We create our own reality using the tools of the universe, the elements of nature, and our will. The professor has all the resources he needs to create the formula for manifestation. His white lab coat indicates his purity of intent. The green board represents the growth he has achieved. He is creating right now, using what he has learned. His references are scientific and metaphysical, esoteric and mundane. They have led him to the same conclusion. There are no limitations as the infinity sign (the figure eight on its side) in his formula suggests. The triangular symbols for the elements—fire, water, air, and earth—are also present in the equation. The solution to the formula is the symbol of the merkaba, the vehicle for transcendence which he actively pursues.

In a reading, this card represents that active participation is needed to create what you desire. Everything else has already been provided. The solution is going to come. It could also indicate that the situation you are in is your own creation. If that is not a desired situation, you have the ability to change it. Do, not want. Be active.

KEY 2
WISDOM

KEY WORDS:
> HIDDEN KNOWLEDGE
> SECRETS

Sometimes wisdom is elusive and must be sought. The reader consults the Tarot seeking knowledge and understanding. The cards lay face down on the cloth before her, not yet ready to reveal themselves. Her left or receptive hand rests upon the deck so that she might draw from or tap into the secrets inherent there. The gold curtain suggests the presence of the Divine which surrounds her. Her necklace, the equal-armed cross represents the truth she seeks. The layout cloth is purple, denoting mastery. The design is in the shape of a merkaba, a vehicle of enlightenment.

In a reading, this card represents that the answers you are looking for are hidden. Keep looking and you will find them. Make sure you are asking the right questions. Ask and you will receive. Spiritual guidance is indicated. You are not seeing the entire picture. Additional information is needed. Secrets may be revealed to you or kept from you.

KEY 3
CREATIVITY

KEY WORDS:
FERTILITY
BIRTH

We are all creators. The pregnant woman uses her creativity to design a nurturing space for her unborn child. She embodies creative expression and wears purple to enhance her imagination. She is a free spirit. Her bare feet demonstrate her connection to the earth and that she is well grounded. The green walls symbolize growth and abundance. This mother-to-be freely uses her mind, body, and spirit to create. The wallpaper border she is applying has a baby block design with the letters of the DNA strands (GATC), the building blocks of life, where all creativity is manifest.

In a reading, this card represents a fertile period where creative energy is flowing. It could also represent a physical pregnancy or the birth of new ideas, new undertakings, and endeavors leading to growth and abundance.

KEY 4
LAW

KEY WORDS:
UNIVERSAL LAW
IMMUTABLE

There is an order to the universe that is immutable like the stars and the planets that the armillary charts. The gardener takes a moment to appreciate the natural order that he oversees. It is only through his diligence that order is maintained. His companion is the animal nature in the world that must adhere to natural law. It is domesticated here and has no choice but to comply. The armillary is supported by a stone pillar representing the foundation for the law. The formal design of the hedges suggests the geometric building blocks of the universe. Anything upsetting that natural order is trimmed back by the gardener. He carries the tool he needs. He wears the colors of the sky and earth.

In a reading, this card represents that the universe is working the way that it should be. If you are having problems, you are resisting universal law. Don't fight it. Trust that the law is working and work with it. Accept things as they are. You have a strong foundation that will always support you.

Key 5
Tradition

Key Words:

ORTHODOX THOUGHT
DOGMATIC PRINCIPLES
CULTURAL NORMS

Tradition has a place in everyone's life. Blind tradition however is limiting. The building represents the foundation of unyielding tradition that influences all societies. Orthodox thought and dogmatic principles need to be questioned for relevance as a society changes, and to enable that change to occur. Blindly following cultural norms in rigid adherence does not allow for growth or change. The colored glass in the windows stands in contrast to the cold structure of the stone symbolizing that the potential for enlightenment is always present even in the most rigid circumstances.

In a reading, this card could represent a need to break with tradition or to establish new traditions. It could suggest being too influenced by conventional thought or brainwashed by another's dogma. It may be a situation where others are judging you or you are judging others for being outside cultural norms.

KEY 6
UNION

KEY WORDS:

LOVERS
CONNECTION TO DIVINE

The philosophy of the Tarot is expressed by Key 6. Within everyone there is a union of conscious and subconscious which reaches for the superconscious. This union exists on every level. The man represents the conscious mind. His left hand is receiving the earth's energy. His right hand connects with the left hand of the woman. She represents the subconscious mind. He looks to her for his link to the Divine. Her right hand reaches out to the universe which represents the superconscious. Their union symbolizes the cycle of spirituality. The conscious can only reach the superconscious through the subconscious. The Divine is reached through prayer, meditation or contemplation, not through thought alone. When the mind focuses on the Tarot images a link to the superconscious is engaged opening the mind to unlimited possibilities.

In a reading, this card could represent a union of body, mind, and spirit or a union with a lover, a business partner, or a spiritual guide. It could also represent a stronger connection to spirituality. Reach for the balance of body, mind, and spirit.

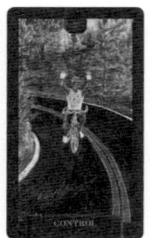

Key 7
Control

Key Words:
Will
Self discipline

True control comes from within. The biker is experiencing a moment of self discipline. He controls the bike with his will, not with his hands. His carefree expression indicates that use of will is not laborious. There are seven stars on his shirt repeating the Pleiades pattern from the previous card.

In a reading, this card represents control. There is either the need for more control in your life or too much control is present. Relax and allow your inner will to guide you. Travel may also be indicated.

Key 8
Fortitude

Key Words:
INNER STRENGTH
SELF AWARENESS
CONFIDENCE

Strength is not only physical. There is also strength that comes from the mind and the spirit. When all three are harnessed in unison, no goal is unattainable. Through his discipline, the martial artist has been able to channel his inner strength. Determination is seen on his face. Confidence can be observed in his stance. He is self aware. His white uniform symbolizes the purity of his thought and intent. These qualities are available to all of us.

In a reading, this card represents inner strength. Do not doubt that you have what it takes to achieve your goals. It could represent someone who is experiencing these doubts which often manifest as lack of confidence.

Key 9
Guidance

Key Words:
Seeker
Counsel
Knowledge

We are seekers. Guidance is found in many ways. The figure here is a student. His yellow shirt suggests that he is actively engaged in the intellectual process. He is seeking outside of himself for answers. He looks up in contemplation as he internalizes the knowledge he has gained. The library's open design reflects his open mind. This is a place of collected knowledge. The physical resources he uses are before him on the table. The lamps' illuminating shades, in the form of merkabas, represent the ethereal sources which are also available to him. The merkaba is a vehicle for transformation and so is knowledge. As we learn we grow, but knowledge alone without experience is limited.

In a reading, this card represents a need to seek guidance both outside of yourself and within. Guidance is always available. Be open to it.

Key 10
Life

KEY WORDS:
DESTINY
CYCLES
PERSPECTIVE

Life is filled with ups and downs. The riders on the roller coaster cannot see the twists and turns ahead of them, but standing back from the situation, we can observe the bigger picture. The riders may not know where they are going, but they know they can't get off. It is their destiny to complete the ride. Some are enjoying the experience and the excitement of life. Others may be filled with fear. It is their perspective that makes the difference. The building is the starting and ending point which symbolizes the cycle of life. The beginning and ending are the same. The colors of the pennants represent the four elements (fire, water, air and earth) which make up all life. The symbols for each element introduced in Key 1 are repeated in the lattice work of the roller coaster.

In a reading, this card represents the ups and downs of life. A new cycle may be beginning and an old one ending. There may be a need to expand your perspective to see the bigger picture. Accept your destiny.

KEY 11
KARMA

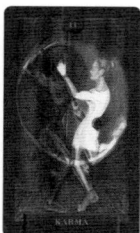

KEY WORDS:
CAUSE/EFFECT
JUSTICE

In the dance of life, a moment has been captured. A man and a woman position their bodies to demonstrate the classic symbol of yin/yang. The man wears black, traditionally feminine and the woman wears white, traditionally masculine expressing the idea of opposites and the balance of positive and negative energies in the universe. The couple indicates that those forces are not gender based. In the dance the partners must support one another to be successful. Balance must be maintained. In life everything balances eventually. That is the principle of Karma, cause and effect. A red curtain offers a backdrop to the dancers. It represents the passionate driving force that fuels the dance. A wooden floor supports the couple. Without stability, passion burns out of control.

In a reading, this card represents true justice prevailing. This could be a legal issue or a personal struggle. Justice here represents what is fair to all parties involved, not what any one person desires. It could also indicate a state of balance or a need for balance in an individual or situation.

KEY 12
CHOICE

KEY WORDS:
SUSPENSION
DECISION

Life is full of choices. Even when we think there are no options, there always are. The driver is suspended in gridlock. He can choose to stay where he is on the current path or take the exit which is open to him. He may not know where that choice will lead but it will be a change. That change may transform his life. This is a process of initiation. The "Quantum" sign suggests that there are no limits to the possibilities. The "Exit" sign is illuminated indicating that he knows what to do. It is uncertain whether he is willing to do it. The rearview mirror suggests that what is in front of him and what is behind him are the same unless he chooses change.

In a reading, this card could represent that a period of stagnation exists. You may decide to stay in this cycle or to take the steps necessary to transform your life. The choice is yours. It could also represent a time to suspend decisions. Not acting is still a choice.

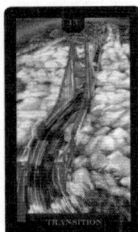

KEY 13
TRANSITION

KEY WORDS:
CHANGE
PASSAGE
TRANSFORMATION

We are continuously moving through passages in our lives; one stage to another, one cycle to another. Without these changes growth would not be possible. The bridge, seen from above, represents this type of transition. Its golden color symbolizes the divine influence that ensures all changes result in transformation.

In a reading, this card represents that change is coming or has occurred. If it has not occurred, its influence can already be felt. This change could be dramatic. It can occur on internal or external levels or both.

KEY 14
DISCERNMENT

KEY WORDS:
EQUILIBRIUM
HARMONY
BALANCE

The costumed acrobat stands solidly on one foot, confident in her ability. Her focus is on the task at hand. She walks the tightrope of life. One false step and she tumbles to her peril. She shows no signs of fear because her judgment is sound. She puts one foot in front of the other assured that her life is in balance. Her costume, the white owl, suggests the wisdom that her philosophy represents. The two-toned bar she holds symbolizes the balance of esoteric and mundane energy in her life. Silver reflects the intuitive energy of the moon and gold the active principle of the sun. This equilibrium is spiritual in nature as one aspect does not overshadow the other but works together in harmony.

In a reading, this card represents that discernment or good judgment is needed. This card suggests a link to the Divine. Use your intuition. Focus on the task at hand. Choose wisely. When you are balanced and focused the path will become clear. A spiritual presence is offering guidance.

KEY 15
MATERIALISM

KEY WORDS:
ILLUSION
DECEPTION
ADDICTION

Society is addicted to materialism. Value is placed on the gratification achieved through material attainment rather than spiritual fulfillment. This addiction manifests on many different levels. All are illusions. Within the garish apartment, the host feeds his guests' addictions through false satisfaction, artificial enjoyment, and delusional pleasure. On the glass table are drugs, money, and weapons. The man on his left is totally oblivious. The woman is willing to do anything for more of what the host offers. Everyone in the apartment is there for the same reason, the false promise of material pleasure. There are no personal connections here. What they feel is a deception. The host looks at the drugs, his tool of control. He doesn't care about the people, only his power over them.

In a reading, this card represents deception. You could be deceiving yourself or someone could be deceiving you. What you believe to be true could be an illusion. This card could also indicate an addiction is influencing the situation. Reevaluate your surroundings and find your own truth.

KEY 16
INTERVENTION

KEY WORDS:
DISRUPTION
ENLIGHTENMENT
TURNING POINT

Life is full of surprises. Those surprises come in a variety of ways and aspects. They are big and small, positive and negative. It is not as important what happens to you as it is how you react to it. Change is constant and inevitable. The family rushes from their home after a tree has fallen on the house. This event is an unexpected change in their lives. The foundation of their security is shaken (the house), so their initial reaction is shock, confusion, and fear, which is understandable. It may bring about positive opportunities they have yet to discover if they remain open to them. This change is universal in nature so it affects everyone in the family, even the dog.

In a reading, this card represents an undeniable disruption in your life. There may be no visible or apparent warning. It comes out of the blue. This is an opportunity to make different choices. Recognize that you have control over how you react. Re-evaluate your situation with an enlightened eye. This is a turning point. Life will never be exactly the same.

KEY 17
MEDITATION

KEY WORDS:
INSIGHT
INSPIRATION
HIGHER SELF

Meditation is a link to our higher selves. Looking within opens us up to the realm of possibility where insight, inspiration, creativity, strength, wisdom, and infinitely more reside. The meditator, shown here in the lotus position, seeks to draw from that inner pool. Her pose and the purple cushion symbolize mastery. Her confidence supports her. She knows she will find what she seeks. That symbolism is repeated in the color of her clothing. The gold tassels on the pillow represent the divine influence which is always present.

In a reading, this card represents the need to look within for answers. You may find what you seek there. Benefit would be gained from meditation. Know yourself.

KEY 18
INTUITION

KEY WORDS:
PERCEPTION
IMAGINATION

Through intuition we connect with the creative or subconscious mind. The woman's gaze is drawn to the crystal ball illuminated on the table before her. The ball is just a tool to focus her perceptions and release her imagination. She is really looking inward where her answers will be found. The color of the cloth and the clothes she wears are purple indicating mastery of the subconscious. She wears gold hoops in her ears. The circle is a symbol of infinity. The energy she connects with is never ending. We are always connected to that energy whether we perceive it or not.

In a reading, this card represents a need to pause and examine the situation. You should trust your feelings. Tap into your creativity and use your imagination for the answers you seek. Something hidden is uncovered or may need to be uncovered.

KEY 19
ILLUMINATION

KEY WORDS:
LIBERATION
JOY

True joy is the liberation of the spirit. The sun, representing masculine energy, shines down upon the rider and his horse illuminating their freedom. Nothing is hidden. They are empowered by the lack of constraints. The white horse symbolizes purity.

In a reading, this card could represent that positive energy surrounds the situation. Use this energy for liberation or empowerment. Enjoy your freedom. Everything is as it seems. This card also could represent good health and healing energy.

KEY 20
AWARENESS

KEY WORDS:
AWAKENING
RENEWAL
CONSCIOUSNESS

Sometimes we don't see what is right in front of our faces. Even the most mundane setting can offer a spiritual awakening. In the midst of this crowded celebration, one participant sees more than the others. She is conscious of a shooting star crossing the sky. It is her opportunity for spiritual awakening or renewal if she sees it for what it is, a gift from the universe.

In a reading, this card represents a spiritual awakening or renewal of the spirit. Be conscious of your surroundings. What you are looking for is there.

Key 21
Completion

Key Words:
Integration
Mastery

The student from Key 0 has now become the teacher. Life is a series of cycles. One cycle in her life is completed. She is teaching the truths that the Tarot reveals. She wears purple, the color of mastery. Earth tones surround her representing her firm foundation in her subject. Her left (receptive) hand is raised toward the wisdom of the Tarot. Her right (giving) hand holds her deck. She is freely giving the knowledge that she has learned. The same layout cloth is on the table as seen in Key 2. It is in the shape of a merkaba, a vehicle of enlightenment and integration. The teacher has integrated enough information about the Tarot to enlighten others.

In a reading, this card represents that a cycle is complete and another one is beginning. You have mastered an aspect of your life. It may be time to share or teach what you have learned.

ELEMENTS

The Elements are comprised of four suits: Fire, Water, Air, and Earth. Each suit is numbered from One to Ten and includes a family unit.

FIRE – RED

Fire is symbolized by the color red. Each of the fire cards are surrounded by a red border. It is associated with the direction south and the season of summer, both denoting its warmth. The fire cards depict dynamic leaders of industry who create and draw success to them with the power of their own will. They represent energy, strength, authority, and ambition.

WATER – BLUE

Water is symbolized by the color blue. Each of the water cards is framed by a blue border. Water is associated with the direction of west and the season autumn, the time of harvest. The nature of water is illusive. It is difficult to prevent its natural flow. Water sustains us, showing us its healing qualities. It represents all emotions. It washes and cleanses. Within the water cards we find those who celebrate life. We find friends and lovers who follow their instincts and move with the flow of the universe. Some resist that flow, holding on to emotional pain, rather than releasing it.

AIR – YELLOW

Air is symbolized by the color yellow and each air card has a corresponding yellow border. Its direction is east and its season is spring, both symbolizing its sense of renewal. Air is vital to our survival yet is seldom seen or heard. Its influence can be physical but most often it is beneath the surface of our awareness. Air rules the mind, the intellect, abstract thought, and knowledge. Air can be uplifting like a kite held aloft by cheerfulness and optimism. Air can be destructive as well. Using thought alone without feeling is building a house without a foundation. A strong enough wind will blow it away. Within the air cards we find a variety of thinkers. There are those who use the knowledge they have gained for their own benefit, and those who find themselves trapped by thought, unable to feel. They are students and teachers of rationality, thought, justice, movement, independence, cleverness, clarity, and truth.

EARTH – GREEN

Earth cards can be identified by their green borders. Its direction is north and its season winter. These both represent a lack of light, like the safety and security of the womb. The earth is our home. It is our source of solidity and stability. The earth cards represent growth, stability, abundance, patience, strength, and endurance.

Family Unit

Within each of the four Elements there is a family unit of Child, Youth, Mother and Father.

The Child represents the Element expressed in its infancy. It is the awakening of the attributes of the Element. These cards often represent children who embody these qualities. The Youth personifies the energy of adolescence within each Element. It is the expression of passion, emotion, thought and devotion before it has the opportunity to mature. These cards often represent young people or people expressing immaturity.

The Mother characterizes the matured Element in the reflective nature of the feminine. Her character is influenced by the subconscious, intuitive and emotional psyche.

The Father characterizes the matured Element in the active nature of the masculine. His character is influenced by the conscious, logical and physical psyche.

ONE OF FIRE

KEY WORDS:

PASSION
ENERGY
POWER

The sun, surrounded by the darkness of space is the ultimate essence of the element Fire. It sustains all life on earth.

In a reading, this card represents a powerful new beginning that exhibits a great deal of energy, momentum that is driven by creativity and passion, or the strength to harness or utilize this force.

Two of Fire

Key Words:

NEW ENTERPRISE
HOPE

Hope is a light that dispels the shadows of doubt. The merchant is holding the scissors at the ribbon cutting ceremony for his new lighting store. He is anticipating success. The mayor joins the crowd around him to wish him well. The merchant has done a lot of work to get here and is proud of the results. Some of the light fixtures in the store can be found in other cards, including the merkaba lamp from Key 9, Guidance.

In a reading, this card represents a new enterprise or beginning. The preliminary work is finished. Be proud of what you have accomplished and have hope for the future. The outcome will be favorable.

Three of Fire

KEY WORDS:

REALIZATION
SUCCESS IN BUSINESS

The hope expressed in the Two of Fire is now realized. The merchant has a successful business and is experiencing prosperity. The store is full of satisfied customers and smiling employees. He has used his passion to turn a dream into a reality.

In a reading, this card represents achieving a goal. Your hard work has paid off. This success could be in business or any other endeavor.

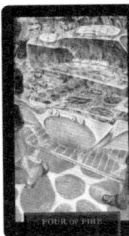

FOUR OF FIRE

KEY WORDS:

CELEBRATION
ABUNDANCE

A summer barbecue is one of the ways we celebrate. The grill laden with food and the people having a good time indicate the joyfulness of the occasion. Abundance is evident.

In a reading, this card represents that a time of celebration is at hand. Recognize the abundance that surrounds you in whatever form it may take. Enjoy.

FIVE OF FIRE

KEY WORDS:
CONFUSION
TURMOIL
COMPETITION

Life can be confusing and chaotic. The ball players' competition has gotten out of control. Fierce determination is expressed on their faces. It only creates more turmoil. One player has fallen. Red, the predominant color, symbolizes the intensity of their energy which they are uselessly discarding. As long as the game lacks structure or focus the players are at risk.

In a reading, this card could represent a situation out of control. Calmly refocus your attention. There may be a need for structure within in your environment. Competition has clouded your judgment. It may also represent the inner turmoil of a conflicted mind.

Six of Fire

Key Words:
- Leadership
- Victory
- Triumph

Leadership comes in many types of roles. This leader, the torchbearer, strides confidently with the torch of victory lighting the way for others. A crowd has gathered out of respect and admiration for her accomplishments. They cheer her on. She is a symbol of the best of the human spirit. She wears the color red signifying her passion to succeed, and white for her purity of heart. A true leader knows that victory is shared, contributing to the success of the whole.

In a reading, this card represents success. This is a moment of triumph and joy. Others may look to you for leadership or a position of leadership may be offered. Celebrate your victory.

SEVEN OF FIRE

KEY WORDS:
PRESSURE
ADVERSITY

We must accept the pressures that come with life. The celebrity walks the red carpet of success and seems to be enjoying his notoriety. His smile does not tell the whole story. He is not able to see the carpet because the flashing lights are overwhelming. It is a continuous struggle to maintain his position. The paparazzi represent the adversity that comes with any situation and can be a catalyst for failure.

In a reading, this card represents a period of adversity. You could be struggling to maintain a position or a situation. Don't give in to the pressure. If you are doing what you want, persevere.

EIGHT OF FIRE

KEY WORDS:
ENERGY
MOVEMENT

In a blazing display of color and light, fireworks fill the night sky. They symbolize the powerful movement of energy.

In a reading, this card represents intense energy surrounding a situation. If this energy is not focused it could burn out or become destructive. You need to utilize this energy now because the intensity won't last. You could be expending too much energy at this time or more energy is needed.

NINE OF FIRE

KEY WORDS:
SECURITY
ISOLATION

Security is comfortable if it is not self limiting or isolating. When you trade liberty for security, you will have neither. The gated community is a safe haven for its residents. Its keypad entry represents limited access. The fire forged metal gate indicates cold, subdued passion. Its bars could become a prison.

In a reading, this card represents a need for protection, not isolation. You may need to limit access to insure security.

TEN OF FIRE

KEY WORDS:
OVERWHELMED
BURDENED

Solutions don't always show themselves immediately. Don't give up even if you feel like you are not making progress. The drivers bottle-necked in a traffic jam cannot see over the hill. They don't know what the problem is, much less the solution. Frustration builds without hope which leads to anger and agitation. They feel trapped and overburdened. The predominant color of red in the card symbolizes the intense energy that could lead to an explosive situation.

In a reading, this card represents being stalled. You feel like you are not making progress. Something may be in your way that you are not seeing. Don't give up. Organize your burdens. Ask for help. Find out what the circumstances really are and then deal with them.

Child of Fire

KEY WORDS:

IMMATURE PASSION
OBSESSION

The Child of Fire is mesmerized by the images of the video game he is playing. His focus is intense but could be fleeting. The passion that drives his determination is immature and could turn to obsession. He ignores the light offered by the window. The only light he sees is from the TV. He wears red, the color of energy, which he has not yet learned to control effectively.

In a reading, this card could represent a person (male or female) or a situation. The person is singularly focused or even obsessive. They may display misdirected or undeveloped passion. Although immature, their passion is sincere and powerful. With direction, they can accomplish anything. The card could also represent a situation where more focus is needed or too much focus is being applied. Walk away from obsessions. Do not waste energy unproductively.

YOUTH OF FIRE

Key Words:
RAW PASSION
IMPULSIVE

The Youth of Fire exhibits the raw passion that drives his life as he roars down the road on a hot summer day. His sunglasses represent blinders that do not allow him to see clearly where he is going. The bike, embossed with the flame emblem represents energy that he thinks is under his control. But it could quickly go out of control or run out of gas as the Youth burns out of energy. Youthful passion can be ill spent.

In a reading, this card could represent a person (male or female) or a situation. The person is reckless, impulsive, or immature. His passion is not yet productively directed. In a situation, you might not be seeing clearly what you are creating in your life. You should stop and think before making any decision. Do not blindly rush in to a situation. This card could also represent a need to exhibit spontaneity.

MOTHER OF FIRE

KEY WORDS:

CREATES SUCCESS
STRENGTH
MATURE PASSION

The Mother of Fire is a mature, dynamic leader. She is driven by her fully developed passion to serve and lead others. The candidate wears red which symbolizes strength. She confidently greets her supporters in the role that she loves to play. She is sure of her victory because she has always created her own success. She stands above the crowd.

In a reading, this card could represent a person (male or female) or a situation. The person is someone who is driven by passion to create success. She is a strong leader who is sure of herself, dynamic, and outgoing. She sometimes may appear cold because part of her agenda is maintaining the role she plays. The card could also represent a situation where strength is needed for victory. You create your own success. Mature or fully developed passion is called for.

FATHER OF FIRE

KEY WORDS:
ATTRACTS SUCCESS
FOCUSED PASSION
POWER

The Father of Fire is a successful leader of industry. He is driven by his focused passion to attract success. He brings energy to every endeavor he participates in. His opulent office reflects his accomplishments. It is in a skyscraper on top of the world. From this height the people below him seem small representing the distance he places between himself and others.

In a reading, this card could represent a person (male or female) or a situation. The person is someone who is driven by a passion to succeed, a dynamic leader. He could be indifferent to personal relationships because he is so focused on success. The card could also represent a situation where energy and passion is needed or too much is being spent. Don't burn yourself out. It could also represent success especially in business. You could be called upon to lead others.

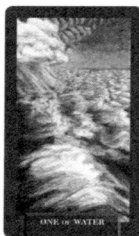

ONE OF WATER

KEY WORDS:
UNCONDITIONAL LOVE
DEEP EMOTION

The sea, expressing its many aspects flows from calm to chaotic. It nourishes all life.

In a reading, this card represents the beginning of a new awareness that is emotionally powerful. It also symbolizes exploring your own emotional depths. Unconditional love is indicated.

Two of Water

KEY WORDS:
PARTNERSHIP
COMMITMENT
LOVE

A successful partnership enhances life. Each participant encourages growth in the other. The moon shines upon two lovers. They stand in the water, gazing into each other's eyes. The couple reaches out to one another to bond their commitment. Blue is the predominate color representing emotion.

In a reading, this card represents the forming of a new beneficial partnership or recommitment to an existing one. It could be love or business or any type of endeavor.

THREE OF WATER

KEY WORDS:
CELEBRATION
FRIENDSHIP

Celebrating with friends is a great way to relieve the stresses of life. The three women are enjoying time together and toasting the occasion. The busy restaurant bustling around them reflects their hectic lives. They are taking a break from that world to focus on each other. The blue candle at the center of the table symbolizes their emotional freedom.

In a reading, this card represents a favorable time. There is an occasion to observe or a celebration is coming. Make time to be with friends. There may be a need to celebrate you. This card could also indicate too much celebration. Don't overdo it.

FOUR OF WATER

KEY WORDS:
OPPORTUNITY

Life continuously offers opportunities. Sometimes we choose not to see those opportunities around us. The self absorbed young man walks only in his narrow world. He chooses not to see the activities going on around him which beckon him for engagement. The recent rain adds to his illusion that this scene offers him nothing. He splashes through his emotions as if they weren't there.

In a reading, this card represents missed opportunities. Open your eyes and look around. What you seek is already there. The universe always provides what we need. It could also indicate that an offer is about to be made and you should anticipate it. Do not close yourself off to the world around you.

FIVE OF WATER

KEY WORDS:
REGRET
DISAPPOINTMENT
ATTACHMENT

Regret inhibits our ability to learn from the past. The former athlete relives old triumphs by looking through his yearbook. He regrets the loss of his fame and is attached to the image of what he once was. As long as he feels his best days have already occurred, they have. The predominant color is blue, suggesting the intensity of his emotions. He only sees disappointment. He should learn from the mascot of his youth. Dolphins never swim backward.

In a reading, this card represents not being able to move forward. Stop reliving the past. Let go of your emotional attachment. Release disappointment. There is a future and it is time to start moving toward it.

Six of Water

KEY WORDS:
SHARING
INNOCENCE
CHILDHOOD

The innocence of childhood makes every experience a new discovery. The boys are sharing the simple wonderment of nature. The delight on their faces is unmistakable. The two stand barefoot in the water, the element of emotion. They do not hide their feelings. They wear the color blue to emphasize their emotional freedom. The frog is the focus of their attention. It is at home in the water and on the land suggesting a balance of emotion. They have the opportunity to grow into that balance.

In a reading, this card represents an opportunity to share your feelings. Be in the moment. Just play. You could be reconnected with childhood friends or memories or have feelings of nostalgia that need to be addressed. You could be dealing with something that has happened in your past or repeating a past behavior.

SEVEN OF WATER

KEY WORDS:
DREAMS
IMAGINATION
BELIEF

To the young dreamer anything is possible. In his world, he is captain of the ship. He cannot fulfill his dreams yet, just like he can't fill the hat, but that doesn't keep him from believing.

In a reading, this card represents that it is time to believe in your dreams and take steps to make them come true. Let your imagination flow. Daydreams can become delusions when we do not act upon them. This card could also represent the need to pay closer attention to dreams when you sleep. They may be offering you guidance.

EIGHT OF WATER

Key Words:
COMPLETION
TURNING POINT

The artist is satisfied that his work is finished. He has turned away from it and is putting up his tools. He is taking with him only what he needs. There is sadness in letting go but he will create again. It is time to move on. The fountain represents that this is an emotional release.

In a reading, this card suggests a need to let go and move on. It is a turning point in your life, an emotional release. Don't look back. Be satisfied that your work is finished. Complete projects.

NINE OF WATER

KEY WORDS:
CONFIDENCE
FULFILLMENT

When we believe in ourselves, we get the opportunity to live our dreams. The captain has fulfilled the dreams he had as the child from the Seven of Water.

In a reading, this card represents confidence. You may not have enough right now or you may be overconfident and need to evaluate your situation. Take the necessary steps to fulfill your goals. You have what you need.

TEN OF WATER

KEY WORDS:
HAPPINESS
LOVE
FAMILY

Time spent together as a family is a rare treasure. The happiness is evident on the parents' faces as they watch their children play. They are all touching the water, connected by the emotion of love.

In a reading, this card represents a happy, contented, lighthearted period. Savor the moment. This card could also represent a family gathering or successful family relationships. It could be the family of your future.

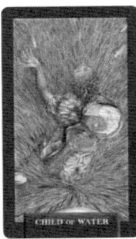

CHILD OF WATER

KEY WORDS:

SENSITIVITY
AWAKENING EMOTIONS

The Child of Water is sensitive and creative. Water, seen here as rain, represents emotion. The Child reaches out to the rain symbolizing his curiosity about that part of himself. The guitar represents a tool to express feelings. The yin and yang on its cover is an expression of balance showing that it is a constructive outlet for his blossoming emotions. The grass he stands in represents growth that is just beginning.

In a reading, this card could represent either a person (male or female) or a situation. The person is sensitive, gentle, emotionally naïve, curious, and spiritual. This person may need to be nurtured and gently guided to express their creativity. The card can also represent a fragile situation. Someone in the situation may be acting immaturely. Or you may need to look at a situation with child like wonder rather than adult cynicism.

Youth of Water

Key Words:

OUTPOURING OF LOVE
EMOTIONAL INTENSITY

The Youth of Water celebrates life. He is in love with love. The blue waves represent emotion. He is a romantic dreamer who rides them without fear. Even though his emotions may crash he does not care or is not aware. He is along for the ride. The white surfboard that supports him represents the purity of the Youth's emotions. His intent is pure but irresponsible. The right or giving hand is in the water to express his need to give love.

In a reading, this card could represent either a person (male or female) or a situation. The person is someone who celebrates life to the fullest and at times is reckless with his emotions and the emotions of others. It could suggest an irresponsible lover. The card can also represent an emotional situation that may be unwise or a new love coming into life that is transient. Proceed with caution or just enjoy the ride.

MOTHER OF WATER

KEY WORDS:
REFLECTIVE
SUBCONSCIOUS
HIDDEN EMOTIONS

The Mother of Water is reflective and introspective as she stares out of her cabin window. She holds her cup close to her chest just as she holds her thoughts within her own heart. Her emotions, represented by the oversized cup, are impossible to ignore. Yet the cup covers her heart, to keep her deepest feelings hidden. The rain on the window further emphasizes the emotional veil through which she sees the world. She chooses to live in a cabin, preferring isolation. Her comfortable, light blue sweater reflects her gentle soul.

In a reading, this card can represent either a person (male or female) or a situation. The person is a dreamer or a romantic who leads with her emotions. She is difficult to get to know because she keeps a lot of herself hidden. She is more at home in her subconscious than in the ordinary world. The card can also represent a situation where reflection is needed to determine if decisions are being based solely on emotions. Look within. Emotions need to be released before a decision can be made.

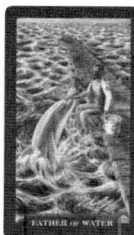

FATHER OF WATER

KEY WORDS:

NURTURING
EMOTIONALLY CONNECTED
HEALING

The Father of Water is a creative, gentle man. He is a nurturer and a healer. He sits above the water, the symbol of emotions. He understands those emotions and is able to share them with others. That understanding is symbolized by his feet in the water. His right or giving hand reaches out to the dolphin. The dock that supports him stretches out over the water. The Father's emotional maturity allows him to feel comfortable surrounded by the sea.

In a reading, this card could represent either a person (male or female) or a situation. The person is emotionally mature and available. He is creative and gentle, perhaps a healer who is not afraid to share his emotions. The card could also represent a situation where nurturing is needed. This type of healing could come from within or in the form of another person or guide. You could be called upon to share your healing energy with another.

ONE OF AIR

___
KEY WORDS:
CLARITY
TRUTH
INTELLECT
___

Wind, the physical expression of the element air, races through the golden sea oats on a New England coastline like our thoughts race through our minds. Air gives life.

In a reading, this card may represent a new idea, a new truth, a new thought or clarification of an existing thought or idea.

Two of Air

Key Words:
Responsibility
Decision

It is difficult to make a decision when you can't see the options. The girl at the fair is playing a game of chance. She chooses to cover her eyes rather than aim at the target. She believes she is giving up responsibility for her actions. However, she has already made a choice. The two yellow balloons symbolize the alternatives open to her. She uses her intellect to worry about the outcome rather than to see these options. No one else can help her with these decisions, just as the carnival barker will not help her win the game.

In a reading, this card represents a need to look at your options. You are not seeing clearly what needs to be done. Make an informed decision. Take responsibility for your actions. Know that there are no wrong choices.

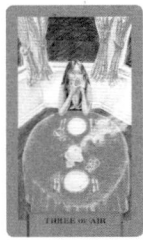

THREE OF AIR

KEY WORDS:
DISAPPOINTMENT
SEPARATION

Expectations can often lead to disappointment. The shocked look on the young woman's face expresses her distress. She expected a romantic evening that didn't take place. Disappointment is separation from your desires. Yellow, the color of thought, is the predominant color in the card suggesting that the way she is thinking has created her sorrow. She did not choose the situation, but she has chosen her unhappiness. The extinguished candle indicates her loss of hope.

In a reading, this card represents a separation from something or someone you desire. There is a need to rethink your situation. Perhaps your expectations are misdirected. How long you suffer the disappointment is your choice. This experience could be the best thing for you.

Four of Air

KEY WORDS:
REST
HEALING

There are times in our lives when we need to rest and gather strength: physically, mentally, emotionally, and spiritually. The boxer is in between rounds. There is nothing that he needs to do right now. Those around him are supplying his needs, offering encouragement, and tending his wounds. This is his opportunity to heal. His yellow shorts suggest that his activity is more mental than physical at this time, but the fight is not over.

In a reading, this card represents a need to rest or take time out so that healing can occur. Gather your strength for what is to come. Accept the assistance being offered.

FIVE OF AIR

KEY WORDS:

TEMPORARY VICTORY
DECEIT
DESTRUCTIVE THOUGHT

Victory gained through deceit is fleeting. No one is a winner. The salesman's tactics are less than scrupulous. Under these conditions he will not be successful. His gain is only temporary. The predominant color in the card is yellow, representing the intellect, which the salesman has manipulated for his own gain. He tells you what you want to hear. His truth shifts like the flags that blow freely in the breeze above his head. He is not harnessing the true power of the intellect.

In a reading, this card represents that caution is advised. Examine your decisions carefully. Read the fine print. Be aware of who you are dealing with. Someone around you is being dishonest with you. It also could represent a temporary victory brought on by deceit. This card could fall if you are deceiving someone else or even yourself.

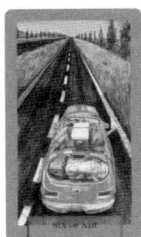

SIX OF AIR

KEY WORD:
JOURNEY

Today's Journey is the life that we lead every day. We make choices and decisions. We have new beginnings and leave the old behind. The people in the car have taken a leap of faith to a new beginning. The car is packed with their belongings. They are taking everything with them so there is no going back. Like the geese above them they are following their instincts. This will lead them in the right direction. The yellow car indicates the positive use of intellectual energy. The paper airplane that the child holds out of the window symbolizes the playfulness of freedom.

In a reading, this card represents a new step or the next step in *Today's Journey*. This change is positive. Let go of the past. It could indicate a trip or a move.

SEVEN OF AIR

KEY WORDS:
THEFT
DECEPTION

If we create our own reality, then nothing can be stolen from us without our consent, whether we are conscious of it or not. Be aware that thieves lurk in all kinds of places and seize the opportunity to take advantage of our vulnerability. Theft can come in many forms. Physical items, energy, or even thoughts can be stolen. Here the thief is a student who is obviously cheating on an exam. Watching from above is the school mascot, a yellow eagle, poised to snatch its prey. Yellow is the color of the intellect. The predator in this case is stealing knowledge. Light casts an uneven shadow on the room. The situation is out of balance. One student's feet are planted firmly on the floor. The other's feet are not grounded.

In a reading, this card represents something being stolen from you or taken without your conscious awareness. It doesn't have to be something physical. It could be mental, emotional or spiritual. Caution is advised. You may be unknowingly taking something from someone else.

EIGHT OF AIR

KEY WORDS:
DESPAIR
FEAR
IMPRISONED

Fear is a self-imposed prison. The woman on the couch is wrapped in despair. Her posture suggests she is unable to see any way out of her fear. The gloomy atmosphere is reflective of her dark attitude. She wears grey, the color of doubt. She has placed multiple locks on her door further signifying her self exile. If she could look beyond her desolation and raise her head, she would see the yellow hot air balloon floating outside. Yellow is the color of thought. The balloon represents the uplifting of thought which could offer her freedom.

In a reading, this card represents feeling trapped in a situation. This prison is self-imposed and you must look within yourself for the way out. Be creative in looking for the answer. Change your thoughts. Do not become overwhelmed by fear. Lift yourself up.

NINE OF AIR

KEY WORDS:

WORRY
SLEEPLESSNESS
TRAPPED

The woman is as caged as her bird by her own thoughts of worry. She can't see a solution to her problems. There is a solution to every difficulty if you are not clouded by your mind. The consequence of the answers her mind creates causes more worry. The bills spread before her represent the stack of problems that are keeping her awake. The empty cup represents the empty solutions of the mind. Air is the element of the intellect represented here by the color yellow.

In a reading, this card represents worry or sleeplessness. Action is indicated. Separate yourself from the situation so that you can see it more clearly. Deal with problems one at a time so that they won't overwhelm you. Every problem has a solution. Help may be needed for a sleep disorder.

Ten of Air

Key Words:
Renewal
Perspective

For every ending there is always a new beginning. Butterflies represent transformation. Their presence among the destruction signifies that this is an opportunity for renewal. The predominant color is yellow symbolizing the positive perspective needed for rebirth.

In a reading, this card represents that the worst is over and it is time to look forward to a new beginning. This is a process of renewal. You may need to change your perspective. Don't focus on the negative. Focus on the opportunities.

CHILD OF AIR

KEY WORDS:
NEW IDEAS
OPTIMISM

The Child of Air is just beginning to learn how to fly. The yellow kite is a perfect symbol for her thoughts. A change in wind could make the direction different at any moment. It could fly even higher or come crashing down without warning. Whatever the outcome she is enjoying the process. Her thoughts have not yet been colored by restrictions or limitations.

In a reading, this card could represent a person (male or female) or a situation. The person is naively optimistic. She may also be flighty, jumping from one idea to another. Her thoughts are pure and her ideas could change the world. In a situation, grounding or focus may be needed. A new idea or thought could take flight. Let yourself go. Brainstorm for new ideas. There's always an answer. Be optimistic.

YOUTH OF AIR

KEY WORDS:
DARING
RECKLESS
INDEPENDENT

The Youth of Air is daring and adventurous. She is sometimes even careless and reckless. She shows no fear as she leaps off the cliff because she feels she is immortal. She will adapt quickly to whichever way the wind blows. She reacts swiftly to adversity by overcoming the challenge. Her yellow suit indicates the boldness of thought which guides her. She utilizes air (her intellect) to sustain and support her. The white glider represents innocence. Her lack of experience does not deter her. The sky is her limit.

In a reading, this card could represent a person (male or female) or a situation. The person is independent, intellectual, daring, and adventurous. This person's analytical skills are hampered by lack of experience, which can make them reckless. In a situation there may be a need to give thought to a current condition. Think about what you are doing and be prepared. Do not act spontaneously. This card may also represent that it is time to take some risks.

MOTHER OF AIR

KEY WORDS:
TRUTH
INTELLECT
JUDGMENT

The Mother of Air personifies truth as she presides over the court. She uses her intellect to separate fact from fiction. The courtroom is her domain and she takes her job very seriously. Her position is one of power and control. The raptor at the window symbolizes the ability to see every detail. Like her, nothing escapes its gaze.

In a reading, this card could represent either a person (male or female) or a situation. The person is not swayed by emotions but uses intellect to discern the truth. She could be perceived as harsh or stern if lied to. Experience has taught her to be strong and smart. In a situation the card could also represent the need to find the truth. Look at the details. Do not let your emotions affect your logic. Use what you have learned to make your own judgments.

FATHER OF AIR

KEY WORDS:
ANALYTICAL
DETACHMENT
INTEGRITY

The Father of Air is a goal oriented, critical thinker. Being airborne, he is literally detached from the earth. The pilot is in control. His cool, analytical thinking produces the proper action to fly the plane. The controls, highlighted in yellow, represent his attention to detail. The passengers and crew trust his integrity to keep them safe.

In a reading, this card could represent a person (male or female) or a situation. The person is cool and emotionally detached. It may be difficult to break through his demeanor. Appeal to his logic. He could be an excellent negotiator and detail oriented worker. He could be controlling because he believes he is right. In a situation you may need to look at the details to find the truth. There may be a need for detachment from the situation or you may be required to get more involved. Be honest with yourself. Take control.

ONE OF EARTH

KEY WORDS:
ABUNDANCE
GROWTH
GROUNDING

The Earth is shown reflecting the lights of the universe. The planet is the ultimate representation of this fertile element. It supports all life.

In a reading, this card represents a new cycle of growth beginning. It may suggest a need for grounding which is a practical focus on the task at hand. Abundance is indicated.

Two of Earth

Key Words:
Juggling
Balance

Are we not all jugglers? The worker in the busy diner is being pulled in many different directions. Taking orders, making change, and pouring coffee are part of her job. Her daughter, doing homework at the counter, also requires attention. Balancing everything is not easy, but she is determined to accomplish it all.

In a reading, this card represents the need for balance. You are juggling too much and need to simplify your life. This could effect situations, people, money, or emotions. It is your choice to be the juggler. How long can you keep it up? This card could also represent that there is a need to manage a situation better.

Three of Earth

KEY WORDS:
RECOGNITION
ARTISTRY

It is important to recognize your talent. The artist, Christopher G. Wilkey (illustrator of *Today's Journey Tarot*) stands proudly with his work at the art gallery. He is receiving the recognition he deserves. Some of the art from the deck is displayed on the wall behind him. The cast bronze sculpture beside him is his artistic interpretation of a merkaba. Art is his vehicle of expression.

In a reading, this card represents recognition. Your talent may or may not be recognized at this time. If you are getting the recognition you deserve, be proud of it. If not, seek it. You may need to recognize your own ability. Tap into your creativity which may be stifled. This card could also represent that you need to recognize someone else's talent and encourage them in the arts.

FOUR OF EARTH

KEY WORDS:
SELF ABSORPTION
SELF SATISFACTION

We are part of the material world but sometimes we forget that we are more than just physical. The woman in the mirror has material richness. The stone she prizes covers her heart symbolizing that she is closed off to everything else. She admires her own reflection. She sees the outward appearance of all she has but nothing below the surface. She wears a green dress which represents growth and abundance. However the dead weight of the fur coat entraps her.

In a reading, this card represents that self reflection is needed. You may be holding too tightly to material things. You could be stingy with your emotions, time, or energy. It could also represent a need to save. Inner soul searching is required to evaluate your situation. Make certain you are seeing beyond your own needs.

FIVE OF EARTH

KEY WORDS:
Loss
Grief
Stagnation

For every ending there is another beginning. The woman cannot see beyond her grief. She sits in front of the stone monument focused only on what she has lost. The monument symbolizes cold, hard, unchanging limitation. The feather which floats down behind her represents the opposite. It is hope, lightness, and freedom. From this position her back is turned to the feather.

In a reading, this card represents a period of stagnation. You may have suffered a loss. It is time to move on and recognize what else is being offered.

Six of Earth

KEY WORD:
CHARITY

There is a difference between asking and harassing. The driver at the busy intersection is clearly annoyed by the solicitors. He feels like he has no choice but to give. The option of when and what charity to support should be his, not theirs. The green bucket represents balanced giving.

In a reading, this card represents giving without expectations. Give because you want to without obligation and without expecting anything in return. You have enough to share. This card could also represent receiving a gift. Do not expect others to give to you. Ask, don't harass.

SEVEN OF EARTH

KEY WORD:
PATIENCE

The winter season is a time of dormancy while we wait for spring. The girl is also waiting as she sits by the mailbox in anticipation of a letter. She knows the message will come because she has done everything necessary to ensure its delivery. The mail box is the vehicle of information. Her green scarf represents the growth that the message will provide when the time is right. She is patient.

In a reading, this card represents the need for patience. Everything has been done to ensure a successful outcome. It is just a matter of waiting for the cycle to be completed.

EIGHT OF EARTH

KEY WORDS:
SKILL
EFFORT
PROSPERITY

We create our own prosperity. Positive thoughts alone are not enough. We have to put forth effort. The jeweler works at his trade, a skill that must be acquired. The tools spread out before him represent his accumulation of knowledge. The optivisor that he wears symbolizes the focus needed to create success. He doesn't loose sight of his goals. The jewels show his connection to the earth and yet are the colors of the chakras. This indicates his spiritual nature which allows creativity to flow.

In a reading, this card represents acquiring a new skill or trade or using the knowledge you already have. Focus. You could turn your talent into a business with the right tools. Apply yourself creatively. Prosperity is indicated.

NINE OF EARTH

KEY WORDS:

ABUNDANCE
INDEPENDENCE
SECURITY

To control a force of nature it is necessary to have no doubt of your ability. The beautiful horse is the embodiment of earth's power. The Nine of Earth represents an abundant, independent life that can be obtained through such self-assuredness and the security that comes with it. The master equestrian gently strokes the horse's mane because she knows with physical strength alone she cannot achieve the results she wants. She holds the reigns loosely in her hand. Her affection for the horse is obvious. She is grounded, with both feet firmly on the earth. The colors that she wears and the horse's coat are harmonious with the earth's energy, which sustains her.

In a reading, this card represents that abundance, confidence, and self-assuredness are apparent or required in a situation or person. Independence is indicated as a method of achieving goals. Problems may need to be approached in a different way. Physical strength is not necessary to control your environment and make it secure.

Ten of Earth

KEY WORDS:
LEGACY
BOUNTY
CYCLES OF LIFE

The past is a story that teaches us who we are and it needs to be told. The children sit engrossed in the tale their grandfather shares. Their green clothing shows their desire to grow. He is passing down the family legacy. This is the cycle of life. The meal being prepared is not the true bounty here. The other adults are distracted by the day's activities.

In a reading, this card represents that a legacy is being passed to you. The cycle of life continues. It is your choice how you use this bounty. Look to elders for advice. The answers you seek are offered from your own past. They could have occurred in another lifetime.

Child of Earth

KEY WORDS:
STUDENT
GROWTH
LEARNING

The Child of Earth is a student. She seeks growth and stability like the natural world she studies. At the Science Fair she is learning about her environment. She learns from experience and must see to believe. It is through the pursuit of knowledge that she grows.

In a reading, this card could represent a person (male or female) or a situation. The person is studious. They may be going to school or need to go. They enjoy learning and the steady progress of education. In a situation this is a period of learning. You may be going to school or training for a new job. Growth is indicated. Embrace it by accepting something new.

YOUTH OF EARTH

Key Words:
STABILITY
PRODUCTIVITY

The Youth of Earth is stable and productive. He shares his love of the earth with others by guiding them through the cave. He is a goal oriented, hard worker. He is focused on his work almost to the exclusion of everything else. He wears green layered over the color yellow to show that his intellect is suppressed by his devotion to labor. Like the formations in the cave that he reaches out to, the Youth of Earth will endure. He is slow to change.

In a reading, this card could represent a person (male of female) or a situation. The person is a well grounded, hard worker. It could also indicate a workaholic who could be perceived as emotionally distant. In a situation there may be a need to focus on work or career. A change in a work situation could be needed or coming. It could also indicate too much focus on work or making money. Discernment is required to know what changes need to be made.

MOTHER OF EARTH

___

KEY WORDS:

NURTURING
FERTILITY

The Mother of Earth is a nurturer. She respects the environment and all of its creatures. Like the earth itself she supports those in her world. She is the physical caregiver for the polar bear cub. She realizes nurturing is required even in the coldest climate. She wears no protection from the cold, willing to sacrifice her own comfort. Her green scrubs stand out like the persistence of life in the harshness of winter. The infant cub represents fertility and growth.

In a reading, this card could represent a person (male or female) or a situation. The person loves nature. She takes care of everyone and offers assistance to anyone in need. Sometimes she compromises her own well being in the process. In a situation there is a need to nurture yourself or someone else. Don't exclude your own needs. It is a fertile time and growth is occurring. There could be a pregnancy.

FATHER OF EARTH

KEY WORDS:
ABUNDANCE
ENDURANCE

The Father of Earth surveys his ranch. He is a builder and what he builds endures. As a custodian of the earth, he produces abundance by using the natural elements to his advantage. He works hard. Green is the color of growth and prosperity. Although he takes from the earth, he gives back in equal proportion.

In a reading, this card could represent either a person (male or female) or a situation. The person is a hard worker who creates abundance. He appreciates the environment and draws his strength from it. This person is not complex but stable, grounded and very practical. The card could also represent a situation where growth and abundance is evident. There may be a need for grounding or paying more attention to your work. What you create at this time will endure. Enjoy what your hard work has accomplished.

THE SEVEN-CARD MERKABA SPREAD

The Seven-Card Merkaba Spread is designed to use with *Today's Journey Tarot*. Shuffle the cards and lay them in numeric sequence corresponding to the diagram provided. Place all cards in an upright position. A reading can cover any area of life. It could be spiritual, relationships, career, family, or health. Make a story out of your reading by linking the cards together and describing what they mean to you. Your first impression is the best interpretation. The cards will address the questions or issues and how that situation is likely to turn out. They will also express the positive and negative influences which should be addressed. The cards are not absolute. Everyone has free will to change their future by making a different decision today. What you are predicting is the probable outcome if no changes are made. The meaning of the cards is influenced by their position in the layout and the other cards surrounding them. They are not limited to any predetermined definition.

POSITION #1 ESSENCE
This is the theme of the reading identifying the central question or situation.

POSITION #2 EXPERIENCE
This is the knowledge from the past that is now influencing the essence.

POSITION #3 INFLUENCE
What is presently affecting the person, situation, or course of events.

POSITION #4 OPPORTUNITY
The possibilities for growth offered that can affect the essence.

POSITION #5 POTENTIAL
The probabilities if action is taken on the opportunity.

POSITION #6 PROGRESSION
This is the movement from potential to manifestation if the opportunity is taken.

POSITION #7 MANIFESTATION
What is being created. If the outcome is undesirable make the necessary changes.

Conclusion

From Beginning to Completion another cycle in Today's Journey has passed. May this deck be your companion through the cycles to come and your guide to Expanding Dimensions.

From left to right Ben Perry, Teresa Sue McAdams, John Lavey, Pat Lavey, Bonnie Taylor

ABOUT EXPANDING DIMENSIONS

The members of **Expanding Dimensions** are from Louisville, Kentucky. Our mutual respect for the Tarot and its wisdom compelled us to create this fresh approach to the Tarot's ancient teachings. Thank you for taking *Today's Journey* with us.

About the Illustrator

Christopher G. Wilkey, whose self portrait is in the Three of Earth, holds a B.A. in Studio Art and an Associate of Applied Science in Computer Graphic Design. He first encountered the Tarot as a child in a book from his family's library that dealt with psychic and esoteric phenomena. He lives in Louisville, Kentucky.

Schiffer Books are available at special discounts for bulk purchases for sales promotions or premiums. Special editions, including personalized covers, corporate imprints, and excerpts can be created in large quantities for special needs. For more information contact the publisher:

Published by Schiffer Publishing Ltd.
4880 Lower Valley Road
Atglen, PA 19310
Phone: (610) 593-1777; Fax: (610) 593-2002
E-mail: Info@schifferbooks.com

For the largest selection of fine reference books on this and related subjects, please visit our website at **www.schifferbooks.com**
We are always looking for people to write books on new and related subjects. If you have an idea for a book please contact us at the above address.

This book may be purchased from the publisher.
Include $5.00 for shipping.
Please try your bookstore first.
You may write for a free catalog.

In Europe, Schiffer books are distributed by
Bushwood Books
6 Marksbury Ave.
Kew Gardens
Surrey TW9 4JF England
Phone: 44 (0) 20 8392-8585; Fax: 44 (0) 20 8392-9876
E-mail: info@bushwoodbooks.co.uk
Website: www.bushwoodbooks.co.uk